INTERVIEW QUESTIONS AND ANSWERS...WITH YOUR FUTURE EMPLOYER

How To Answer The Toughest Interview Questions

REBECCA RAMOS

Contents

1. Introduction: 1
2. The Questions   2

Interview Questions and Answers...With Your Future Employer

*How To Answer The Toughest Interview Questions
(130 Interview Questions and Answers To Come Out On Top)*

Introduction:

Even though there is a huge range of potential answers to interview questions, s0me will get you hired and others will get you the boot. We have compiled a list of 130 solid Interview Questions so that you can be prepared for your interview. Each question consists of a potential answer, why it is being asked, and tips to create the best answer for yourself.

LET'S GET STARTED!

2

The Questions

1. **Q: What do you feel you can offer this company that another candidate cannot? Do you possess any special skill sets pertaining to the job duties of this position? (A two part question deserves a two part answer)**

A: I believe I can offer my expertise in the field of (sales, for example) being that I have worked as a sales representative in this area for the past 10 years. Not only do I have the experience needed to succeed in this position, but I get results. I was a top sales representative in my former job and earned top ranking bonuses consistently due to my ability to produce credible leads, which I source myself unless you would like to provide them, and follow through with them and close the sale. What makes me different from other sales reps or candidates is my ability to be assertive while not overbearing. It is my dedication to my position which drives the results I am actually able to obtain.

WHY IS this question being asked?

This is an important question because it details a specific question interviewers would actually want to know. They want to know what makes you stand out from the rest, and why you would be the best candidate for the position. Tell them what sets you apart, and include skills you bring to the table that others may not possess.

TIPS:

Don't drive the interviewer crazy by providing too much detail. Just say enough to get them interested, and supply all relevant information that could be used to make an informative decision based upon the details you have provided. Make eye contact always when answering any questions, and be honest.

1. Q: What type of a degree do you have?

A: I have my _____ in _____ and I graduated from (school) in (year), and earned (honors or awards) while I was enrolled.

A2: I don't currently hold any degree from a higher learning facility, however; I don't believe that will prohibit me from getting the job done right and doing my absolute best for this company.

WHY IS this question being asked?

Employers like to understand how educated you are, which can be very important when applying and interviewing for various positions. This information should also be included on your resume as well, but it's always a possible question which may be asked in person. Be ready, and make sure you tell the interviewer what awards you received (i.e. – Dean's List Honors, et cetera) while in school. If you didn't go to college, again – be honest. Sometimes, the job may require a degree of higher education. Other times, it's not a deal breaker if you don't have a college degree. The employer will surely inform you if one is necessary.

TIPS:

Don't exaggerate. Be honest, and to the point.

1. **Q: Do you have any relevant experience in this line of work?**

A1: I do have experience in this line of work, as I have worked in this sector for (x) amount of years (or months) in my prior job at (name of previous employment/company).

A2: I do not yet have any experience in this type of work, however; I am a fast learner, and am able to pick things up quickly if given some instruction, and from there, I am capable of working well on my own.

WHY IS THIS BEING ASKED?

Employers want to know if you are actually capable of completing the assigned duties and want to know your level of understanding of the position and tasks.

TIPS:

If you have no experience, say so. Lying won't do you any favors, as your boss will quickly learn you really never had the skills to begin with, and you will be dismissed from your position quickly in that case. If you don't have experience, say so with positivity, meaning – say you don't have the required experience, but you are willing to learn and do what you need to do to get the job done.

1. Q: How did you hear about the position?

A: I saw it on/in (website name/newspaper name/job board, et cetera where you found the job advertisement) and decided I would take a chance and apply.

WHY IS THIS BEING ASKED?

Many employers advertise positions with various and multiple venues, some of which cost them a great deal of money. Sometimes, this is a way for them to keep track of whether or not some of these costly websites are worth the advertisement cost. Other times, they are just asking out of curiosity.

TIPS:
None

1. **Q: Can you tell me more about yourself?**

A: Provide the employer with a brief personal history, such as family and whether or not you have children, who will be watching them throughout the day (or night) while you work, and whether or not they are school aged, which is important. Tell your potential employer a little bit about your hobbies, which show them who you are as an intellectual. Don't be too detailed, and don't talk about yourself *too* much. Summarize what you are going to say and have that in mind before going to the interview, as you will undoubtedly be asked this question. Perhaps give a few examples of prior work history which could pertain to the position at hand. Correlate something to say that will incorporate life and employment experience into how you would be the right fit for this particular job.

WHY IS this question being asked?
The employer is trying to get a feel for who you are as a person in general. They want to know a little bit about you intellectually, which can speak volumes in terms of gaining the position. They are also looking to see *how* you

will answer this particular question. Many people aren't well prepared to answer a personal question about themselves, so be sure you think this one through before interviewing.

TIPS:

Honesty is key. Don't be too wordy. Smile, and summarize.

1. **Q: Have you heard of our company before? What do you know?**

A: Yes, I have heard of your company before. I know that you have been in business for (x) amount of years, have (x) amount of employees, and that the company was founded by (name of founder). I know that the company specializes in (whatever they specialize in), and does business (wherever they do business).

WHY IS this question being asked?

Employers want to know if you are doing your research. They want to know just *how* interested you are in the position, and why. They want to hear what you actually know, which should be based on factual evidence gathered via the internet or whatever other source you choose to use.

TIPS:

Do your homework. The internet is your best friend in this case. You have the ability to find out virtually anything you want about a company via the internet. Sites such as Manta.com allow you to input a company name, and research how many employees are currently with the company, the CEO's name, or Founder's name, and even how much the company makes in annual revenue. Use this information to your advantage.

1. **Q: Why do you want to work here?**

A: I want to work here because I respect and admire the company as a whole, I believe in the company's mission, and I think I could bring something wonderful to your company (state some of your skills, but don't overdo it). I hope to grow with the company and offer my support in any area I am needed in. I desire to help the company thrive and grow.

WHY IS THIS BEING ASKED?

Employers are curious as to your motives. If you simply state something such as, "I need money", chances are you won't get the job. They want to know that while you want and need the job, that you are capable of wanting to actually help the company in some sort of way other than for your own benefit.

TIPS:

Be generous in stating you want to help the company,

and want to grow with the company. Typically, employers want to see long term potential, because it costs them money in the long run looking for new employees when someone just decides to up and leave. Make it clear that you intend on sticking around for a while.

1. **Q: Do you believe we should hire you, and why?**

A: I do believe you should hire me, because I am a hard worker, results oriented, dedicated, and put my all into my work. Unlike other candidates, I choose to go above and beyond for my employer and don't only focus on what's minimally due, but I make it the best it can be. I desire to be the best at my position, and I'm not here solely to benefit myself. I generally like helping where I am needed, and for that reason I believe I am worthy of being hired. I also bring my skills in (whatever your skills may be) to the table, and my skills coupled with my desire for success make me a fantastic candidate.

WHY IS THIS BEING ASKED?

Although this may seem like a strange question, employers want to know whether you believe and are confident enough to answer this question with conviction. They want to see you exhibit confidence that you really *are* what their company needs, and therefore should answer as such.

. . .

TIPS:

Show strong confidence in your answer, but not enough to sound arrogant. Give them reasons why they should hire you for that particular decision over other candidates, and ease their mind with the fact that you plan on giving the position your all.

1. **Q: What are your strengths, and weaknesses?**

A: Some of my strengths include my ability to prioritize, work with minimal guidance and instruction, computers (detail which applications you are proficient at), my ability to type (x) words per minute, the level of honesty and integrity that I bring, and my skills at (whatever your skills are). Some of my weaknesses include (state your weaknesses, but keep it to a minimal, ensuring you have spoken more strengths than weaknesses).

Why is this being asked?

Employers want to know your strong points, and your weaknesses. They want to know whether or not you will need someone telling you what to do every few minutes, or whether you are capable of taking the reins into your own hand, and getting the job done. They need to know what your weaknesses are to know if you would be a good fit for the job, and whether its something you can improve on.

TIPS:

To reiterate what is stated above, don't give too many weak points in your answer. Just keep it to one or two, but make sure they are important ones. As an example, you could say, "I don't have much experience in Photoshop, however; I am willing to take classes or work on that if necessary." They like to hear you counteract your weak point with a positive follow up.

1. **Q: Have you received any awards during your tenure in previous jobs?**

A1: Yes, I have received the Employee of the Month award (or whatever award(s) you have received in prior jobs) for my outstanding work ethic and ability to push myself to the limit for my employer.

A2: No, I haven't received any awards, however; I am willing to change that at this opportunity. I wasn't eligible to receive rewards or awards in my previous positions due to (whatever factor went into not getting awards), but I want to prove to you that I am an outstanding employee which you will see once you hire me.

WHY IS THIS BEING ASKED?

Employers want to know how good of a job you have done in previous times and compare that to the current position you are applying for. They want to know how dedicated you are to your position.

TIPS:

Always try to keep a positive focus on things, even if you haven't received any awards. Make it sound like you plan on getting this job and showing them that you deserve awards and that you will be sure to become eligible whilst there.

1. **Q: What was the most challenging part of your previous job?**

A: The most challenging part of my previous job was (whatever the challenge may have been, describe it in detail.) I chose to work through it, and not give up, even when things got really difficult. I am not a quitter, and desired to pursue the challenge until I ultimately beat it, and prevailed.

WHY IS THIS BEING ASKED?

Employers want to know how you will deal with difficult situations when faced with them. Are you going to be afraid and just walk away, leaving things undone? Or are you going to dive in, face first, and tackle the situation at hand when it arises? This is something you need to think about wording applicable to previous adversities you have dealt with in your previous work.

TIPS:

Avoid cowering. Answer this question with bravery. We have all faced difficult things in our positions; be confident in your answer and ensure your potential employer that you are the person to get things done – no matter what.

1. **Q: Do you have a 5 year plan?**

A1: I do. My five year plan consists of (whatever you choose to do within the next five years that is of extreme importance to you, such as buy a car, buy a house, get married, go back to school, finish your degree, et cetera). I would also like to be in a steady position in my career life, growing with the company and succeeding in my goal to help the company attain growth and success.

A2: Although I do not have a set 5 year plan as of yet, I am confident that I will still be working in my position here at (whatever the company name is). I really don't believe in developing a 5 year plan, because (provide a few reasons as to why).

WHY IS THIS BEING ASKED?

Your potential employer would like to know where you see yourself in the future. They want to know how responsible and goal oriented you are.

TIPS:

If you don't have a 5 year plan and have no intention on developing one, provide reasons as to why. Example: I am against 5 year plans because setting goals that far ahead doesn't work for me. The reason being is [provide your reasoning].

1. **Q: What is your ideal job?**

A: My ideal job is [provide details on the position and company, if applicable. Also, provide something positive about why you think this job you are interviewing for may in some way – big or small – correlate with your dream job].

WHY IS this question being asked?

Your employer wants to gain a sense of what you're really aspiring to do, and this may help them make an educated decision as to whether this particular position is right for you. If your dream job is to design clothes, and you are applying for a car wash position, chances are you aren't going to be considered a good candidate because your heart wouldn't be in the work as much as someone else's may.

TIPS:

Be honest, and speak from the heart. Your ideal job is something you would be passionate about, so allow yourself to speak freely to give your interviewer a sense of who you are as a person, and also allow them to make the best decision for the company, and for you.

1. **Q: Why are you planning on leaving your current job?**

A: I am planning on leaving my current job because I feel as though (example) there is no room for growth, or advancement, and that is what I am looking to obtain. I want to provide my skill to a company that respects me as an employee, and I didn't feel I was getting that with my current employer.

WHY IS this reason being asked?

Obviously, this is a major question – one your employer will expect an honest answer to. So, be honest. Explain the reasons why you felt it was time to move on. Don't bash your current employer, just state why you feel your needs as an employee was not being met.

TIPS:

Speak honestly, but do *not* down talk your current boss.

1. **Q: What are you personally looking for in a job?**

A: I am looking to gain new experience, while bringing my already established skill set to the company and put it to good use. I want to work with a company that values my skill, and treats me with the mutual respect I will treat my employer and co-workers with.

WHY IS THIS BEING ASKED?

Potential employers want to know what *you* want before

establishing employment. Keep it simple but make your desires known.

TIPS:

Don't go overboard with detail. Just state the specifics and most important aspects.

1. **Q: Do you have management experience?**

A1: Yes, I have prior management experience in (detail what your experience is in a manager position and for what company).

A2: No, I don't have management experience, however I am willing to learn whatever I need to obtain that role within this company if necessary.

WHY IS THIS BEING ASKED?

Perhaps the employer feels you would be good in a management position rather than the position you are applying for. Or perhaps you may be able to move into that arena eventually, and they want to know how you would handle it and whether or not you have ever done something like this before.

TIPS:

Be honest. Tell your interviewer if you don't feel a

management position would be right for you and state why.

1. **Q: What do you know about this industry?**

A: I know (give prime examples as to what relevant information you have. Provide details as to first-hand experience you have had in the industry.)

WHY IS this question being asked?

THIS IS BEING ASKED because the interviewer wants to know what your knowledge on the industry is and whether or not you have relevant experience to bring to the job.

TIPS:
Be honest, and don't try to provide knowledge or information you don't actually have unless you have your facts straight. If you only have minimal knowledge of the industry, say so. It's better to state minimal knowledge than to make something up and sound like a fool.

1. **Q: Are you willing to relocate for the position?**

A: Yes, I am willing to relocate.

OR

NO, I am not willing to relocate. (If no, provide a reason as to why)

WHY IS this question being asked?

IN CASE of possible openings at other branches, they may need to find someone who is willing and able to relocate.

TIPS:

PROVIDE A CLEAR ANSWER. It's not good practice to say you will need to think about it. The employer may need to know then and there, so this is important. Think about this question before you actually set off to the interview.

1. **Q: Is there anything you would like to ask me or know?**

A: This is where you will ask any questions which you may have had written down regarding the position, the place of employment, your employer themselves, or something you may have been wanting to ask throughout the interview.

WHY IS this question being asked?

THE EMPLOYER IS GIVING you chance to ask things you may be curious about and might want to know.

TIPS:

BE sure to ask anything that's on your mind, but leave personal questions out of the equation.

1. Q: Do you work well with others?

A: Yes, I do work well in either a team environment or with a couple of other people.

WHY IS this question being asked?

THE PROJECT MANAGER, interviewer, or employer would like to know if you would be a good fit to place with their team – especially if most projects are done in a group format. They want to know there won't be any issues with anyone who they hire not being capable of working with others.

TIPS:

Again, honesty is the key. It's important to note that you should be up front if you are unable to work with other people in a team environment, and state the reasons why.

1. **Q: Do you handle constructive criticism well?**

A: Yes, I do. I have learned that it helps me to grow in my profession, and become a better employee overall. I have also noticed that it helps me to find the flaw in my work where I may have previously thought I was doing well.

WHY IS this question being asked?

THIS QUESTION IS IMPORTANT, because nearly all employees will at some point provide you with constructive criticism. You need to learn how to take that criticism and implement it for the better of your work and position.

TIPS:

Learn to love criticism. It helps to mold you as a person – both in the workplace, and in your everyday life.

1. **Q: Tell me about a time where you've gone above and beyond your job description at work.**

A: Example: After working at my last job for about two months, we began attending trade shows. At one of the trade shows, my boss had received a phone call with bad news about a family member. The timing of the phone call was about 10 minutes before a scheduled TV interview with a local news channel. I took the initiative to speak on our company and products on behalf of my boss, with her permission of course, due to the face that she was emotionally distraught. I was nervous, as I had zero experience in doing something like this previously, however; I felt it was time to go above and beyond my experience and comfort zone for the sake of the company.

Why is this question being asked?

YOUR BOSS WOULD LIKE to know what kind of person you are. They want to know that in the heat of the moment and when things get tough, you've got their back. That's important to them.

TIPS:

YOU SHOULD THINK of your most valiant deed that you have ever done for a previous boss, and use that example as your answer. Keep it to the point while providing enough detail that they understand the velocity of the situation and why your acts were so important to the company.

1. **Q: How do you handle working with someone who doesn't do their job and pull their weight?**

A: I have worked with people like this in the past. For a while, I let it go and hadn't said anything to anyone about it. Eventually, I began pulling their weight for them. I realized I shouldn't have to be the one doing the other person's job while they were getting paid for it and so I eventually spoke with that person in a calm manner and explained my feelings. If that wouldn't have worked, though, I would have gone and spoken with my supervisor about it.

WHY IS this question being asked?

DURING DIFFICULT TIMES at your job where an employee may take advantage of a new team member, your boss wants to know you won't just sit back and allow that to happen. They want to know you will take action and do something about it.

TIPS:

. . .

KNOW who you're dealing with. If the person's reputation is to be that of a violent or easily agitated persona, you should always speak directly to the boss regarding the issue. Safety always comes first.

1. **Q: Everyone makes mistakes. Tell me about a time where you messed up on the job. How did you deal with the situation?**

A: One time, I made the mistake of inputting a meeting date at the right time on the wrong day. I realized this the day before the meeting was actually due. I corrected it on the calendar, and spoke to my boss about it. She wasn't upset, and thanked me for correcting the mistake.

WHY IS this question being asked?

YOUR BOSS WOULD LIKE to know they can trust you in the event you mess up – which everyone does. They want to know you will do the right thing.

TIPS:
   As always – honesty is the best policy. Be honest!

1. **Q: Have you ever had to be hard on**

someone in your job? If so, how did you handle that?

A: I have not had to do that.

OR

I HAVE HAD to do that, and although I didn't like it, it was something that had to be done. I spoke to them in a firm tone, but wasn't mean or insulting. I said what needed to be said and then we came to a mutual understanding.

WHY IS THIS BEING ASKED?

YOUR BOSS WANTS to know if you have ever had to be the one to make hard decisions, and how you went about it.

TIPS:

DON'T GO TOO much into detail, just state the facts.

1. **Q:** If you were asked to do something by either your Supervisor or boss that you felt

uncomfortable with, how would you handle that?

A: Depending upon what was asked of me, and the level of offense I felt, I suppose my reaction would be different. If I was asked to do something I was morally not okay with, I would speak my mind to my supervisor and be honest about it. If I was asked to do something that somehow broke any laws, I would tell them I'm sorry, but I cannot do that. It all depends on the situation I was faced with.

WHY IS this question being asked?

THIS QUESTION IS BEING ASKED to test your character.

TIPS:
Always be honest in a situation like this.

1. **Q: What are you biggest workplace pet peeves?**

A: I can't stand when I bring lunch to work, and other people help themselves to my personal lunch that's labeled with my name. I also don't like when people don't clean up after themselves, or take supplies from my desk without asking. Other than that, I have no real pet peeves.

WHY IS this question being asked?

THIS QUESTION IS BEING ASKED because again, your interviewer is testing your character.

TIPS:

Give an honest answer, but don't have a running list of things you can't stand!

1. **Q: Are you good about meeting deadlines?**

A: Yes I always meet deadlines, no matter if I have to work late to finish them or bring home work with me.

WHY IS THIS BEING ASKED?

MEETING DEADLINES IS important to a company. Ensuring they are hiring the right person for the job who will go above and beyond and show initiative is important.

TIPS:

MAKE the interviewer see that you are responsible and understand the importance of deadlines.

1. **Q: What was the most difficult circumstance you have dealt with in your personal or work life, and how did you manage to handle it?**

A: (Provide insight as to the most difficult circumstance you have ever dealt with, and explain how you handled it and got through it. Since this answer will vary from person to person, this answer serves as a general guideline on how to go about answering)

WHY IS this question being asked?

YOUR EMPLOYER WOULD LIKE to know how you deal with difficult events in your life, so they can better understand how you will likely deal with situations that arise at work.

TIPS:

EXPLAIN and be sure to include feeling in your response. Feelings can be extremely persuading.

1. **Q: If you saw illegal acts being committed in your place of employment, what would you do and how would you handle it?**

A: I would go directly to the authorities and speak to them regarding the information I possessed. Under no circumstances am I willing to work in or participate in a work environment that could potentially have a negative effect on me in any way, either work related or otherwise. Also, I would resign from my position as soon as possible.

WHY IS this question being asked?

YOUR EMPLOYER WANTS to know how honest you are.

TIPS:

BE AS HONEST AS POSSIBLE. Chances are your employer will never participate in anything illegal, and if they were to, you more than likely wouldn't want anything to do with being a part of that company, anyway.

1. **Q: What is your desired salary?**

A: I am looking to get $x per hour (or, per week).

WHY IS this question being asked?

THEY WANT to know what your expectations are and whether they can meet your requirements or not. This is an important question.

TIPS:

AIM HIGH. Say at least $1.00 over what you really want per hour. Chances are, you will get the amount you are asking for, or $1-2.00 per hour less than your quote. If you aim higher, you will not necessarily be disappointed when the amount you ask for is turned down and re-negotiated.

1. **Q: What was your salary or hourly wage within your last position?**

A: I received $x/ per hour (or) per week at my last place of employment.

WHY IS this question being asked?

THEY WANT to be able to compare your recent pay to the

amount you are asking for now. More than likely, this will be confirmed with your previous employer, and also will be evaluated against the skill set you have.

TIPS:

DON'T LIE. Lying to try to get a higher rate of pay will more than likely land a denial on your interview, due to the fact that employers tend to do their research on potential job candidates. They usually do and will check up on you – even if they hire you, and you become an employee. Don't run the risk of losing a job you just got over a silly lie.

1. **Q: Are you interested in receiving company benefits?**

A: Yes, I am interested in receiving health and dental benefits. I am also interested in a 401 (K) plan if you offer that.

OR

NO, I am not interested in benefits – just in obtaining the position. I currently have my own private health insurance.

WHY IS this question being asked?

Interview Questions and Answers...With Your Future Employer

THE EMPLOYER WANTS to know if you would like to be a part of their health and dental plan, as some employers do pay a portion of the cost per month and even match what you pay, and they also need to know for HR purposes so that they can get everything established and ready to go once you accept the position.

1. **Q: How do you see yourself a year from now, professionally?**

A: I see myself in a stable position, hopefully within this company, where I am evolving into a more important job role and growing with the company. I see myself bringing success to this company in every way I can, and contributing all of my time and attention while I am here to the betterment of this company.

WHY IS this question being asked?

THE EMPLOYER WANTS to know how long you plan on sticking around, and what your professional plans are. Some employers want temporary employees, others are looking for those who are ready to be in it for the long haul.

TIPS:
Definitely throw something in there about seeing your-

self at the company you are interviewing with as this looks good for your long term projected goals.

1. **Q: What would your previous employer say about you?**

A: I believe my previous employer would state that I am a hardworking individual who always went above and beyond for the company. I believe he would also say I am honest, trustworthy, always ready to help however I can, and reliable. He always told me how much he appreciated how I put my all into my work, and even took on various projects to help him alleviate the burden of doing it alone.

WHY IS THIS BEING ASKED?

THE EMPLOYER WANTS to get a sense of what others would say about you in your professional life. Commentation from previous employers is important. This tells the employer a lot about your character in the workplace.

TIPS:
Be honest.

1. **Q: What would your previous co-workers say about you?**

A: I believe my previous coworkers would say I am easy to work with and get along with, and can always offer a helping hand to others where it is needed.

WHY IS this question being asked?

THE EMPLOYER again wants to get a sense of what it's like working with you, and what type of a working environment you will bring to the office.

TIPS:
Provide specific examples of things previous co-workers have said about you if possible, and name drop as well. This may be checked on.

1. **Q: Have you been arrested previously, or do you have a criminal past? If so, what for?**

A: No, I have not been arrested at any point.

Or

. . .

YES, I was arrested for _____. (Explain and state when you were arrested)

WHY IS this question being asked?

IT'S important for employers to know whether or not you have a criminal history, especially in certain businesses.

TIPS:

ALWAYS BE HONEST. Your background history will most likely be checked. Don't lie!

1. **Q: Do you have reliable transportation to and from work?**

A: Yes, I do. I have a _____.

WHY IS this question being asked?

YOUR EMPLOYER WANTS to know whether or not you will be able to get to work on time every day without reason for excuses such as 'My car broke down'.

. . .

TIPS:

IF YOU DON'T CURRENTLY HAVE a vehicle, state that you will use whatever means to get to work such as a bike, bus, cab or train.

1. **Q: Do you do drugs of any kind or drink alcohol?**

A: No, I do not do any drugs of any kind. Yes, I occasionally have a drink or two.

OR

NO, I do not do any drugs of any kind. No, I don't drink.

WHY IS this question being asked?

ALL EMPLOYERS WANT clean and sober employees. Some employers tend to do drug screenings before hiring you, so be sure to tell the truth.

TIPS:

BE HONEST.

1. **Q: What is your credit score?**

A: State what your credit scores are for the three major credit bureaus – Transunion, Experian, and Equifax. If you don't know, say so.

WHY IS this question being asked?

MANY EMPLOYERS NEED to have employees working for them who have good credit scores – especially in the business and financial world.

1. **Q: Would you submit to a credit check?**

A: Yes, I would.

OR

NO, I would not. (State the reasons why)

WHY IS this question being asked?

LIKE THE ANSWER to the above question, many employers need to keep a running record of employee credit scores for the credibility to the company.

TIPS:

Don't be nervous. If you are told your credit is bad, just move on to the next position you are seeking employment at – and work on fixing your credit for your own good.

1. **Q: What is your ideal working environment?**

A: I would like to work somewhere that is peaceful, quiet, and where I am able to work on my own most of the time. I would rather work alone than with people.

OR

I WOULD REALLY LIKE to work in a team environment where there is constantly something going on, as I love the chaos and bustling environment.

WHY IS this question being asked?

THE EMPLOYER WANTS to know what type of a worker you are, to be able to tell if the position will be right for you.

1. **Q: How long do you think it will take to get into the swing of things within this position?**

A: I think it will be a fairly quick process and I don't believe I will need more than week to get into the swing of things.

WHY IS THIS BEING ASKED?

YOUR EMPLOYER WANTS to know how long it will take for you to be able to do your job efficiently.

1. **Q: Do you think you will need any training?**

A: I believe I will be okay without training due to my past experience.

OR

Interview Questions and Answers...With Your Future Employer

I BELIEVE I will need some training, but it shouldn't take much.

WHY IS this question being asked?

THE EMPLOYER WANTS to know how much time you will need for training, and how much.

1. **Q: Are you bilingual?**

A: Yes, I speak English and _____ fluently.

OR

NO, I am not bilingual.

Why is this being asked?

CERTAIN AREAS in the country have a higher rate of Spanish and other speaking residents. It's important for companies to have employees in this area who speak various languages who can break the language barrier. It's not always a factor in every position.

TIPS:

IF YOU ARE NOT BILINGUAL, state that you are willing to learn and receive training or take classes if the company would like to pay for them.

1. **Q: Are you willing to take a language class to learn a foreign language if the company pays for it?**

A: Yes, I am willing to learn! (show excitement)

WHY IS this question being asked?

THIS MAY BE important to the employer.

TIPS:
Show initiative, and express gratefulness to the employer for providing this service to you.

1. **Q: Are you willing to travel for the job to trade shows and other events?**

A: Yes, I am willing to travel as long as the company is compensating or paying for the travel.

. . .

Or

NO, I am not currently able to travel due to _____. If the travel is local, I would consider it.

WHY IS this question being asked?

SOME COMPANIES DEAL with a lot of promotional travel and therefore need employees who are able and willing to travel.

TIPS:

DON'T SAY you aren't willing to travel if you are unable, state that you are unable to and give them a reason why. Whether it's family related (children), or otherwise.

1. **Q: Are you organized?**

A: I am extremely organized and keep everything in order at all times.

WHY IS THIS BEING ASKED?

. . .

NO EMPLOYER WANTS an employee that is unorganized and discombobulated in their daily work life. It looks bad on the employer and makes you look bad as well.

TIPS:

GIVE examples as to how and why you are organized. i.e. I keep an organized file cabinet.

1. **Q: Are you a quick witted thinker?**

A: I am on my toes and definitely think quickly and act accordingly when I need to.

WHY IS this question being asked?

SOMETIMES, split second decisions need to be made in order to make or break a business deal. Being quick witted and ready to act on those decisions for the best possible outcome for the company is something you will need to learn to be good at, and actually act on it.

TIPS:

Don't flat out say 'No, I'm not quick witted'. If you aren't a quick witted thinker, state something similar to the answer above, but include something like, 'I am always working on improving myself'.

1. **Q: Who is your role model, and why?**

A: Why role model is _____ because _____.

WHY IS this question being asked?

YOUR EMPLOYER IS TRYING to see the type of person or people you look up to, and why. This helps them get a better idea of who you are and what you stand for.

TIPS:
Try to keep it to one person, two at the most.

1. **Q: What are your hobbies?**

A: I like to read, listen to music, go to the beach, etc. (List things you actually like to do.)

WHY IS this question being asked?

. . .

YOUR INTERVIEWER IS ATTEMPTING to get to know you as a person.

TIPS:
Be yourself!

1. **What do you think of your last boss?**

A: I think my last boss was a great business man/woman, and really knew how to run the business the right way. I believe he/she is a great person in general.

WHY IS this question being asked?

YOUR POTENTIAL NEW boss wants to know if you harbor any regrets or hateful feelings towards a boss, or see if you will speak ill of them.

TIPS:

DON'T SAY anything bad about a previous boss, ever! This is bad all the way around the board.

1. **Q: What is one thing you have always wanted to do?**

Interview Questions and Answers...With Your Future Employer

A: I have always wanted to go to Europe (example) and visit some of the cathedrals in Rome.

WHY IS this question being asked?

THIS IS a personal question to see a bit of your personality type. Answer truthfully and have fun with this question.

TIPS:
See above

1. **Q: What are three words that you'd use to describe yourself?**

A: Happy, extroverted, and dedicated (examples, say what you think about yourself)

WHY IS this question being asked?

THESE ARE personality questions to get a handle on how you perceive yourself. Answer truthfully.

TIPS: See above

1. **Q: What are you afraid of?**

A: I have fears that don't relate to actual portions of my life. I have no fears about my abilities or work. My fears pertain to things beyond my control, such as natural disasters (tornadoes) and cancer.

WHY IS this question being asked?

THE EMPLOYER WANTS to see if you have any fears or intimidations pertaining to the workload or your capabilities.

TIPS:
Assure your employer that they have nothing to worry about as far as your work is concerned and that you have faith in yourself. Don't look vulnerable.

1. **Q: What kind of car do you drive?**

A: I drive a _____.

WHY IS this question being asked?

ALTHOUGH THIS QUESTION is rather prude, some employers have been known to ask this question – especially in the business and real estate world. Just answer and sound happy no matter what your vehicle is. The employer may believe those who have a nicer car may be more successful as studies have shown.

TIPS:

DON'T SHOW concern or forlorn if your car is less than perfect. Be happy about it, no matter what it is, and show them confidence in your decision to have that car, and give them reasons why you love it.

1. **Q: What is your favorite operating system?**

A: Windows based systems are my favorite, and I prefer them over Macs.

OR

MACS ARE MY FAVORITE SYSTEMS, and I prefer them over Windows.

WHY IS this question being asked?

THE EMPLOYER WOULD LIKE to know if you are capable and easily able to use the operating systems within the office network.

TIPS::

Don't say anything bad about the systems they use, maybe interject the question with a question of your own such as, 'Well, let me ask you what kind of operating systems you use here at the office?' before you provide your answer. Don't lie, but don't speak ill of the systems they use.

1. **Q: Would you think it was strange to teach your boss things you know and are educated on that they don't know?**

A: No, not at all. I would be glad to help and teach whatever and however I could.

WHY IS this question being asked?

PERHAPS YOUR POTENTIAL employer sees something in you they think you could teach them to better their abilities.

. . .

TIPS:

OFFER TO HELP however you can.

1. **Q: If you were to win the lottery today, what would you do with the money and why?**

A: I would invest in a company and some profitable stocks, put money away for my children to attend college, pay off my student loans, and pay off any debt I owe. (This is just an example; provide a responsible answer)

WHY IS this question being asked?

THIS QUESTION IS a test to see how responsible you are financially.

TIPS:

GIVE A RESPONSIBLE ANSWER. Don't say something like, 'Party!' or 'Blow it all on a weekend Vegas trip!' That will not impress the interviewer.

1. **Q: What did you always want to be when you grew up?**

A: I always wanted to be a doctor. (example; provide your own response)

WHY IS this question being asked?

PERHAPS YOUR EMPLOYER wants to see how well you planned for your future and why you did or didn't stick with your childhood dream.
   Tips:
   Use honesty.

1. **Q: Who is your favorite author?**

A: My favorite author is Dean Koontz. If I can't find a Koontz classic, I stick with Steven King. (example. Provide your own response.)

WHY IS this question being asked?

BOOKS SAY a lot about a person's personality. This is a psychological question for the most part.

. . .

Interview Questions and Answers...With Your Future Employer

TIPS:
Keep it to a minimum as hard as it may be in terms of providing a name. One or two authors suffice.

1. **Q: If you were an animal, what kind would you want to be – and why?**

A: I would want to be a horse in the wild west, running free through the fields and open land of Montana. If not a horse, then a dolphin as they are gentle, free roaming creatures with sweet dispositions. (provide your own examples and give reasons to back them up).

WHY IS this question being asked?

THIS IS a mental question to evaluate your thought process.

TIPS:
Keep it to two animals, if it is hard to pick just one.

1. **Q: If you close your eyes, can you tell me how many windows and lights are in this room?**

A: Yes, there are two windows and two lights.

WHY IS this question being asked?

THE INTERVIEWER WANTS to know how observant you are.

TIPS: Evaluate your surroundings when you arrive to the office and enter the interviewer's office or room.

1. **Q: I want you to sell me this pen.**

A: This pen is a very special pen. It's unlike any other of its kind. It has features which other pens cannot compare to. It's exceptionally made with care and quality, which ensures it has been put together well and will not soon run out of ink. It writes perfectly every time, so you won't have to go look for another pen to do the job that this one will do every time. There has been nothing else like it, and more than likely, there will be copycat versions of this same pen – but none can beat or come close to this exact pen. Everyone is going to want one, but this one can be yours right now. You can have one before the rest of the world, and be the envy of all of your peers. Everyone will want to know where you got this extraordinary pen from. All you need to do to buy is one pay $199.00 and it can be yours, no questions asked, right now. This pen will show your peers how successful and important you are. You deserve to write with something of this exceptional quality. You've earned it. You're worth it.

WHY IS this question being asked?

ALTHOUGH A STRANGE QUESTION, this is a typical question asked at many sales related interviews. They will pick up a random object, and as simple as it is, they need you to pitch them a sale. They are looking for someone who is capable of convincing, and making that sale. They want you to tell them why they should buy that item right now, and use persuasion to do it.

TIPS:

BE PERSUASIVE! Sell the item, no matter what it is. Make them want to buy what they may already own.

1. **Q: If someone was to write a book about your life, what would you think they should title it?**

A: I believe it should be titled, 'Undefeated' (example)

WHY IS this question being asked?

THEY WANT to know how you would label your life.

TIPS:

USE ONE WORD TO describe your life.

1. **Q: If you were stranded on a desert island, what two things would you have with you?**

A: A phone and water.

WHY IS this question being asked?

YOUR EMPLOYER IS TRYING to see the types of things you would have on you at all times, to evaluate your personality type and responsibility level.

TIPS:

USE common sense when answering this question. Nobody would actually have a walkie talkie or Television with them at all times (or a boat). Therefore be sure to answer with something you will always have on you.

Interview Questions and Answers...With Your Future Employer

1. **Q: If you had only three months to live, how would you spend that time?**

A: I would spend it doing everything that made me happy, and leave behind no regrets.

WHY IS this question being asked?

THE INTERVIEWER IS TRYING to gain insight as to who you are.

TIPS:

THINK this question through before actually interviewing. Answer honestly.

1. **Q: If you could meet any historical figure, who would you choose to meet and why?**

A: I would choose to meet (example) Thomas Edison, as he was a brilliant inventor and incredible man. I respect him highly for his creativity and desire to never give up.

WHY IS THIS BEING ASKED?

. . .

THIS IS BEING ASKED to find out more about your thought process and logical thinking skill.

TIPS:

NONE

1. **Q: Have you ever come up with a solution to a complex problem nobody else could develop successfully? If so, what was it?**

A: I did, actually. I came up with a chart system to keep deadlines organized in a way nobody else had done within that company before. (example)

WHY IS this question being asked?

THE INTERVIEWER WANTS to gain a sense of your potential and abilities.

TIPS:

DON'T GO OVERBOARD on details. If you haven't come

up with a system to solve a problem before that nobody else had, just say so, and be honest.

1. **Q: If you were to get this job, when could you begin?**

A: I would gladly begin as soon as possible – On Monday of next week, I could start.

WHY IS this question being asked?

THE EMPLOYER WANTS to know when you could begin the work. Chances are, they need you to begin as soon as possible. Give an exact date/day as this helps to clarify things for them.

TIPS: Give an exact date/day.

1. **Q: What is the best job you've ever had, and what did you like about it?**

A: I would have to say the best job I have ever had would be running a Non-Profit Organization because I felt as though I were contributing to the betterment of humanity in some small way. Every day I got to make a difference to the lives of children living in Africa, and help raise awareness on Malaria and how real it is, and how many children it affects each and every single day. (example)

WHY IS this question being asked?

THIS QUESTION IS BEING ASKED because your employer is generally curious as to what you enjoy doing in the workplace, and why.

TIPS:

Give details, and stay on point. Point out the most relevant aspects as to why you enjoyed the position.

1. **Q: Do you feel as though you are a responsible individual? Why?**

A: I do believe I am a very responsible individual because of the fact that I am a mother, for one thing. I raise four children and ensure their day to day lives are in order, doctor's appointments are made and met, and they are fed, clean, clothed, happy and healthy. Due to my extensive experience at being a mother, I have gained quite a great deal of experience at being responsible. Aside from that, I would say my experience in the workplace has given me a great deal of responsibility as I managed and directed important aspects of the company, and my experience within this company gave me the ability to make sure I was

responsible at all times. Because of these factors and more, I think I am very responsible. (example)
Why is this question being asked?

YOUR EMPLOYER WANTS to know how responsible you think you are, how honest you are, and why you think so.

TIPS:

GIVE detailed life experience as well as relevant job experience.

1. **Q: What is the average time frame it takes you to complete an assignment?**

A: That depends on what the assignment is. Normally, I am able to complete the assignment or project within a designated time frame without taking extra time. We can discuss that when the time comes.

WHY IS THIS BEING ASKED?

THE INTERVIEWER IS TRYING to get an idea of how long it normally takes you to complete the designated work to make sure you would be a good fit for their team.

. . .

TIPS:

DON'T GIVE an exact time frame, because deadlines and topics vary per project. Simply state you are able to get the project done within a reasonable time frame.

1. **Q: What is your favorite thing to do at work on a daily basis?**

A: My favorite thing to do is check the e-mail every morning, and respond to all of the prospective clients. (example)

WHY IS THIS BEING ASKED?

THIS IS BEING ASKED so the interviewer can get a better idea of the types of things you are really into on the job.

TIPS:

JUST BE HONEST!

1. **Q: Could you ever see yourself running or managing a business?**

Interview Questions and Answers...With Your Future Employer

A: Yes, I could. I believe I have the management skills necessary coupled with the experience necessary in order to run a business properly and get things done.

OR

NO, I don't think management would work well for me. I feel as though I am a better worker when not in a management type position.

WHY IS this question being asked?

PERHAPS THE INTERVIEWER has plans down the road and would like to know if you might be a good fit for the position they may be opening up.

TIPS:

DON'T LIE; if you don't like management jobs, simply say so.

1. **Q: How often do you expect pay raises?**

A: I would like to see pay raises at least once per year after review of my performance. If I am excelling with the company and doing a good job, that is when I would expect a raise.

WHY IS THIS BEING ASKED?

THE EMPLOYER WANTS to know your expectations.

TIPS:

BE REALISTIC.

1. **Q: How many hours per day are you able to work?**

A: I am capable of working 6-8 hours per day. (example)

WHY IS THIS BEING ASKED?

THIS IS BEING ASKED because your interviewer needs to know if you are able to work the amount of hours allotted for the position.

TIPS:

DON'T EXAGGERATE. Be realistic in your response, and make it clear how many hours you are ready and willing to work.

1. **Q: What did you go to school for?**

A: I went to college to become a Paralegal, and obtained an Associates of Applied Sciences in Paralegal Studies from ABC University. (example)

WHY IS THIS BEING ASKED?

THIS QUESTION IS BEING ASKED because the interviewer would like to know what you have been trained to do and see if it applies to the job position.

TIPS:

JUST BE HONEST. If you never went to college, just say so. Not having gone to college isn't always a deal breaker and stating the fact that you didn't is better than lying. Your education can always be checked into, and if you were to provide false information and the employer found this out, they would certainly disqualify you from the position.

1. **Q: How many jobs have you had in your lifetime?**

A: I have had four steady full time jobs, and one part time job. (example)

WHY IS THIS BEING ASKED?

THE EMPLOYER WOULD LIKE to know about your employment history.

TIPS:

BE sure to list this information on your resume under experience for the interviewer to look at after the fact. Also, many times your interviewer will go over your resume during the interview and ask you questions pertaining to the information listed, so be prepared.

1. **Q: Name two things you would like to see changed in the workplace, at any job, anywhere.**

A: I would like to see more equality for women to be paid the same as men who do the same job within the same position. I would also like to see health care benefits become more affordable for employees. (example)

WHY IS THIS BEING ASKED?

THE EMPLOYER IS TRYING to pick your brain on what you would like to see done differently. Perhaps this isn't for any particular reason, other than to see your viewpoint on things.

TIPS:

LIST SOMETHING you are passionate about. Think about this one before going to the interview.

1. **Q: Is there anything in particular you would like to ask me?**

A: I would like to know when the company started, and what it was that made the founder want to build a company in this niche. Was it something he was passionate about? Or was it more of a lucrative monetary decision? (example)

WHY IS THIS BEING ASKED?

THE INTERVIEWER IS GIVING you a chance to ask questions pertaining to the job, or themselves. Be sure not to ask personal questions as this is in bad taste.

TIPS:

DON'T ASK ANYTHING PERSONAL.

1. **Q: What are the major points of working in sales?**

A: Sourcing and developing leads, interaction, persistence, and closing the sale.

WHY IS THIS BEING ASKED?

IF THE POSITION is in sales, the employer wants to know you know what sales is all about. Also, they want to know you know how to source and close a sale.

TIPS:

HOPEFULLY, you know a bit about sales before applying for a sales representative position. If you don't, do your research prior to the interview.

1. **Q: Why shouldn't I choose to contact your references, and why?**

A: I wouldn't mind it at all if you contacted my references, in fact I encourage it. However, if I had to provide a reason as to why you shouldn't, I would say my employment history can speak for itself. I have (x) amount of years' worth of experience in this line of work, and my track record will show I have longevity in my positions. This should show the details that are most important, such as long term opportunity potential and loyalty to my employer.

WHY IS this question being asked?

IT MAY SOUND like a trick question, but your interviewer wants to see if you are capable of providing a valid reason as to why they shouldn't need to contact any of your reference points.

TIPS:

DON'T SAY SOMETHING LIKE, 'Well, because contacting references is a pain in their rear end'. Keep things totally professional, and to the point. Give reasons why that aspect is completely unnecessary and relate it to your experience.

1. **Q: Are you easily angered?**

A: No. I tend to deal with situations as they arise, and work them out in a calm manner. It really does take me a lot to get upset. I like to proactively deal with anger, rather than lash out at someone. That's never a solution to any problem.

WHY IS THIS BEING ASKED?

THE INTERVIEWER NEEDS and wants to understand your personality. They need to protect themselves, and their staff, from potentially unwanted behaviors exhibited by new employees.

TIPS:

DON'T SPEAK TOO much on this. Just keep it simple and direct.

1. **Q: If your present employer wanted to offer you more money, would you stay with that company? If so, why? And if not, why?**

A: I wouldn't stay if I was offered more money, because of _____ (state reasons as to why)

OR

I WOULD HAVE STAYED if this was offered to me before I began my job search, because the only reason I was leaving was due to the fact that I needed more money. However, if I was offered more now at the present time, I would politely decline due to new opportunities.

WHY IS this question being asked?

THE INTERVIEWER WANTS to know if the reason you were leaving was due to money, or something else.

TIPS:

BE honest but polite in your answer. There's no need to elaborate too much here.

1. **Q: How many other companies have you interviewed with, and are set to interview with?**

A: I have interviewed with (x) companies, and am set to interview with (x) more.

WHY IS THIS BEING ASKED?

THEY MAY WANT to present you an offer of employment right then and there. Or perhaps, they may just want to get a general idea of how actively you have been pursuing interviews and job searching. This shows your drive.

TIPS:

IF YOU HAVEN'T INTERVIEWED with anyone else, just say so. You may just be starting out on your job search, and they may be the first company you have interviewed with in doing so. No need to make anything up, just be honest.

1. **Q: If we hired you today, what do you think you would direct your main priorities towards in the next week?**

A: If you offered me employment today, I would want to spend the next week learning your systems, computer programs and software, and getting acquainted with life within this office and this company. I would introduce myself to all of the staff and all of my co-workers, and prioritize my list of things to do, so that come Monday of next week, I would know what I needed to work on in order of importance. (Example)

WHY IS THIS BEING ASKED?

PERHAPS THE INTERVIEWER is thinking of choosing you for the job. Be sure to have a well thought out answer developed if in fact this question is posed to you. Prioritize.

TIPS:

YOU SHOULD SAY what is actually feasible for you to do, and don't make false promises of getting right to work if you don't or can't physically begin that until acquainting yourself with the new systems and programs you will be working with.

1. **Q: If one year from now you and I were celebrating the success of something you had taken part in that made this company even greater than it is today, what would that be?**

A: I believe my contribution to working on _____ and _____ would play an impeccable role in that celebration, and I look forward to that celebratory day at this time next year. I know I can make a difference in the projection and future of this company.

WHY IS this question being asked?

SIMPLY, the interviewer wants to know what your mindset is in thinking for the future of the company. Do you have the growth and best interests of the company in mind? Say so.

TIPS:

BE sure to throw something in there that says, 'I can't wait to celebrate that moment with you'.

1. **Q: What are some things you do not like to do in the office?**

A: To be honest, there isn't much that irks me in an office environment. One thing that does bother me, though, is gossip. I will not partake in any gossiping or trash talking, no matter who the person is who is trying to converse with me. If I have a problem with someone, I keep it to myself or take it up professionally with said person myself. (Example)

. . .

WHY IS THIS BEING ASKED?

THE INTERVIEWER WANTS to understand if there is something you don't like to do pertaining to your job.

TIPS:

RATHER THAN BASH JOB DUTIES, state something you wouldn't do professionally within the office environment. The example above dictates an actual event you will not participate in.

1. **Q: Why have you had so many jobs in such a short amount of time?**

A: Due to _____ I have had to change jobs frequently. I don't anticipate this affecting my position here with your company, as I have resolved these obstacles. I am looking for something long term that I can stay and grow in.

WHY IS THIS BEING ASKED?

IT'S A LEGITIMATE QUESTION. The employer wants to know why you have had that many jobs in that amount of time. It concerns employers when they see you haven't held a job for very long.

TIPS:

EXPRESS the fact that you plan on staying in this position for quite some time. Give examples as to why you know you are capable of staying put for a while, and be honest as well.

1. **Q: What do you think about office meetings?**

A: To be honest, it's not my favorite thing to do in the world, however I understand their importance, and it allows everyone to become aware of ongoing work, progress, and situations. Therefore, even if I wasn't mandated to attend and was given a choice, I would regardless, because it's an important aspect of working within a company.

WHY IS THIS BEING ASKED?

PERHAPS THE INTERVIEWER just wants to hear an honest answer, and nothing sugar coated.

. . .

Interview Questions and Answers...With Your Future Employer

TIPS:

BE HONEST, but don't give a sassy answer.

1. **Q: How could you help this company save money?**

A: Aside from using less electricity than I need to, I would choose to not use the printer unless absolutely necessary, saving on toner, electronic, and paper costs. I would also search for ways to be more cost effective in my daily duties, like if there were any money saving services or coupon programs I could implement into the costs associated with my job duties. I would of course run these by you or whoever you deem necessary, and avoid needless spending on company cards by holding myself accountable. (example)

WHY IS this question being asked?

THE EMPLOYER WANTS to know if you have the understanding of how much it costs to run a business, and whether or not you would be proactive in helping them to run it efficiently with less monetary necessity.

TIPS:

THINK of some clever ways you could save money, and use these in your answer.

1. **Q: What are you the best at doing in your trade?**

A: I am the best at writing. I have over three years' worth of experience in various forms of writing, and I am passionate about it. (example)

WHY IS this question being asked?

THEY WANT to know what you feel your strong points are.

TIPS:

THINK of the skill you possess that you are most confident in. Use this as your example.

1. **Q: If you had to remove one amendment from the constitution, what would it be, and why?**

A: I would have to say the right to bear arms. I don't

believe any civilian person should be able to carry guns, only authority figures and military personnel. Regular people don't need to have guns. It causes too much chaos in today's world, and more and more, needless mistakes are happening at the hands of criminals with access to weapons. (example)

WHY IS THIS BEING ASKED?

THEY'RE TRYING to gain access to your thought process and learn a bit more about you.

TIPS:

CHANCES ARE, you won't be asked this question. However, it has been asked by many employers, believe it or not. Have an opinion all your own here. It's okay to speak freely. This is an opinionated question.

1. **Q: What do you consider perfect communication?**

A: Speaking directly, making eye contact, and speaking articulately and slowly enough for the person listening to fully understand and grasp what you're saying. Also, asking if they have any questions for you about what you've said at the end.

WHY IS THIS BEING ASKED?

IS the job you are applying for dealing directly with the public? If so, they want to gain an understanding of how you would speak to potential clients.

TIPS:

USE SOMETHING similar to the provided answer. This is what most all employers are looking for.

1. **Q: Have you ever taken a pen from work?**

A: Yes, I have, accidentally. I did return it as soon as I realized my mistake.

OR

NO, I haven't ever done that, even by accident.

WHY IS THIS BEING ASKED?

TEST OF CHARACTER.

TIPS:

BE HONEST. If you have done this, say it was accidental and you returned it.

1. **Q: What do you normally do with your cell phone when you arrive at work?**

A: I turn it on vibrate, and if it rings, I check to see who's calling for my own knowledge as I have children. If it's their school, I ask permission to give the school a call back, but if it's anyone else, I will let it go to voicemail and deal with it after work. I also don't text while I am working.

WHY IS THIS BEING ASKED?

THEY WANT to know if outside distractions will interfere with your abilities while on the job.

TIPS:

EVEN IF THE interviewer seems laid back, don't say, "I will

answer it if it rings". Tell them you will turn it on vibrate, if not off.

1. **Q: How would you rate my interviewing abilities?**

A: I believe You are very thorough, and are asking all of the right questions. I also appreciate your time, and the fact that you've been courteous and personable during the interview. On a scale of 1-10, I would rate you a 10 for those facts alone.

WHY IS THIS BEING ASKED?

INTERVIEWERS LIKE INPUT on their abilities and also, like honesty. If you don't feel they have done a good job, say so in a nice way and explain why.

TIPS:

DON'T SUGAR COAT ANYTHING, but don't be rude, either.

1. **Q: If you could choose to be anyone in the world for one day, who would it be, and why?**

A: I would like to be _____ because they have contributed _____ to society. They are extremely smart, kind, giving, and _____.

WHY IS THIS BEING ASKED?

THEY ARE LOOKING in depth at the person you are and what inspires you.

TIPS:

CHOOSE CAREFULLY.

Q: Are you efficient with Quickbooks, by chance?

A: Yes, I am. I have (x) years' worth of experience in working with Quickbooks.

OR

NO, I am not. However, I am very willing to learn if you would like me to.

. . .

WHY IS THIS BEING ASKED?

PERHAPS USING Quickbooks is something you will need to do in the position you are applying for.

TIPS:

STATE THE TRUTH, and show a willingness to learn if you are not familiar with Quickbooks.

101.
Q: If you had to choose a song to describe you, what would it be?

A: I would choose _____ by _____ because _____.

WHY IS THIS BEING ASKED?

THE INTERVIEWER IS TRYING to gain perspective as to who you are in a fun and interesting way.

TIPS:

. . .

CHOOSE A WELL-KNOWN song that they would most likely know.

102.

Q: If you were contacted by an investor who had plenty of money to spend, and they asked you to pitch them an idea of your own creation, what would it be?

A: I would pitch them idea I have been working on for a while now, which is _____. I would provide plenty of details as to why they should invest in my idea and product, and sell them the idea harder than I have ever hustled anything in my life.

WHY IS THIS BEING ASKED?

PERHAPS THE INTERVIEWER is curious as to what kind of personal drive you have to succeed.

TIPS:

IF YOU'VE NEVER INVENTED anything or tossed the idea around, come up with something you are passionate about and think about what could help improve that genre in some way.

. . .

103.

Q: When you are driving in your car, what thoughts go through your mind more than any others?

A: My family and things I need to do when I get home or things I want to do with them on the weekend in my time off.

WHY IS THIS BEING ASKED?

THIS IS BEING ASKED because your interviewer wants to know what's important to you, and what your priorities are. Saying things like, 'I can't wait to party this weekend' are not a good idea.

104.

Q: Do you have a good memory?

A: Yes, I do. I still remember things from when I was little, even down to the smallest detail.

OR

MY MEMORY IS PRETTY GOOD, I remember really important things and important dates and meetings, but I don't remember insignificant little details about things.

WHY IS THIS BEING ASKED?

IN PRETTY MUCH ANY PROFESSION, retaining things which were said to you are important for a multitude of reasons.

TIPS:

IF YOU STRUGGLE with memory issues, perhaps try some brain training exercises.

105.
Q: What is the last newspaper you read?

A: The last newspaper I read was the New York Times this morning.

WHY IS THIS BEING ASKED?

MANY EMPLOYERS LIKE to know their potential and established employees are keeping up with things pertaining to the trade they work in.

106.

Q: Tell me how many gas stations there are in the United States.

A: I would estimate there are approximately 130,000 gas stations throughout the United States.

(In actuality, there are 121,000 according to the US Census Bureau therefore that answer is close)

WHY IS THIS BEING ASKED?

EMPLOYERS WANT to see how you strategize. Be prepared to explain why you believe there is that many gas stations. If you had previously read about it, say so. If you compared numbers and used mental math, state the math you use.

TIPS:

SEE above

107.

Q: Say your friend whom you haven't seen in a long time is in town. They call you and ask you to meet for drinks. You make plans for Friday night. Suddenly, a deadline comes up that wasn't anticipated and you need to work late. What do you do?

. . .

A: I call my friend, and reschedule our time slot, or ask if we could meet another time. I would need to make the responsible decision and put work first. It would be unfortunate, but for the best if we were unable to see each other. I would try my best to make it possible to see them in my off time though.

WHY IS THIS BEING ASKED?

THE INTERVIEWER WANTS to know where your priorities lie.

TIPS:
Say what they want to hear, here!

108.
Q: How do you stay safe in the workplace?

A: I don't go into the parking garage alone. I follow proper protocol for using equipment and machinery, and I follow all of the rules set forth by the company. I also use my best judgment when in doubt.

WHY IS THIS BEING ASKED?

COMPANY INSURANCE TENDS to be expensive. They want to know you most likely won't need to file any claims.

TIPS:

USE an answer like the one provided for a happy interviewer.

109.

Q: What is your workplace philosophy?

A: My work is my life. I need my position to support my family. I really put my all into my work, and I treat the company as if it were my own, putting proper care into everything I do.

WHY IS THIS BEING ASKED?

THE INTERVIEWER WANTS to know you care about your job.

TIPS:

STATE REASONS why your work means so much to you.

110.

Q: Are you a good motivator when you see other co-workers slacking or down?

A: I am. I try to cheer them up, offer help if I can, and give them a reason to smile.

WHY IS THIS BEING ASKED?

FOR JOBS where you work in teams, this is exceptionally important. Motivation is key.

TIPS:

STATE SOMETHING similar if not verbatim to the answer.

111..
Q: Are you innovative?

A: I believe I am extremely innovative, and I am always coming up with ways something in the workplace could be improved or become more efficient. I constantly look for solutions to difficult problems, and try to streamline difficult tasks, providing easier solutions for all involved.

WHY IS THIS BEING ASKED?

EMPLOYERS LOVE creativity and input from employees.

TIPS:

STATE how you love to be helpful with suggestions and use your skill of creativity to make things easier. Employers love easier.

112.

Q: What would your best friend say about you if I asked?

A: She would say I am fun, creative, funny, loyal, sappy, a little crazy (in a good way!) and great to hang out with. She'd probably also say I'm a great cook! (throw some humor in there, it's okay this time) (example)

WHY IS THIS BEING ASKED?

THIS TESTS SELF-CONFIDENCE AND CHARACTER.

TIPS:

BE YOURSELF FOR THIS ONE.

. . .

113.

Q: What qualities should a team leader possess, and why?

A: Team leaders should be assertive, loud in terms of making their voice heard without being annoying, organized, well spoken, idealistic, and creative. They should also be able to manage large groups of people, and have the patience to deal with issues that may arise calmly.

WHY IS THIS BEING ASKED?

THE EMPLOYER WANTS to know your thoughts on leadership, and this is also a professional character question.

TIPS:

THINK of great leaders you have read about. Use examples of things they have exhibited in their time as leaders for whatever their position may have been and use those.

114.

Q: Does likeability or respect mean more to you?

A: I would have to say both. I don't think I would like being disliked, however I don't believe I would handle being disrespected well, either. I would like the perfect balance of both, in a perfect world. If I absolutely had to choose, I would choose to be respected.

WHY IS THIS BEING ASKED?

CHARACTER QUESTION

TIPS:

CHOOSE CAREFULLY and word your answer according to whatever you feel you need more.

115.

Q: Is your personality different at work than it is in your everyday life?

A: I believe I am more serious at work, and that would probably be the only difference.

WHY IS THIS BEING ASKED?

THIS IS A PERSONALITY TRAIT QUESTION, which is important to the employer.

. . .

TIPS:

List one trait that differs from your home life to your professional life.

116.

Q: Are you skilled in social media?

A: I am. I have a lot of experience in using Facebook, Twitter, Instagram, LinkedIn and Pinterest.

WHY IS THIS BEING ASKED?

DEPENDING on the position you are going for, this could be important to your daily job duties.

TIPS:

LIST all of the social media networks you have experience with, and provide examples as to why you are experienced there. What have you done on those networks?

117.

Q: Have you ever done something everyone else thought you were unable to do? If so, what was it?

. . .

A: I have! I went to school and graduated as a Paralegal with my Bachelor's Degree. Nobody in my family has ever gone to college, and I was the first one. I was told repeatedly that I would never make it. That pushed me harder and made me want it more. Look at me now! (example)

WHY IS THIS BEING ASKED?

THE EMPLOYEE WANTS to know how well you do when faced with difficult odds and situations. They also want to test your self confidence level.

TIPS:

BE EXCITED to answer this one. Show your enthusiasm in your answer!

118.
Q: Are you a generally happy person?

A: I would say I am a very happy person. I'd be happier if I got this position, though. (example)

WHY IS THIS BEING ASKED?

THERE COULD BE a number of reasons as to why this is

being asked. This could be a self-esteem based question, a character test, or this could be to determine whether or not the employer sees underlying depression related issues, which they may be thinking could affect the insurance rates of the company. State how happy you are, and make sure to mention something about how much happier you would be (even more than you are already) if you got this position.

TIPS:

SEE above

119.
Q: If you were me, would you hire you?

A: Honestly, yes, I would. I believe I am the best candidate for this job because _____ (provide explanation)

WHY IS THIS BEING ASKED?

THIS IS a test of your honesty, and character.

TIPS:

IF YOU WANT THE JOB, say yes.

120.

Q: What are some first impressions you created internally about the office when you arrived?

A: I noticed everything was organized, and well kept. It was very clean. The receptionist was extremely friendly. I noticed there were a lot of plants and flowers, so I assumed the company was very eco- friendly and perhaps even big on recycling. (example)

WHY IS THIS BEING ASKED?

THE INTERVIEWER WANTS to know how observant you are.

TIPS:

BE OBSERVANT UPON ARRIVAL.

121.

Q: What is your favorite quote of all time?

A: "Never, ever, ever, ever give up" – Winston Churchill (example)

WHY IS THIS BEING ASKED?

THE EMPLOYER FEELS it's important to ask this question so they can understand your theory on life and what's important to you. You can tell a lot about a person by the quotes they live by, including intelligence.

TIPS:

IF YOU DON'T KNOW any quotes, look some up on the internet. Find one that fits your theory on life. Learn it, and be prepared.

122.

Q: If you could be a kitchen utensil, which one would you be?

A: I'd be a spoon. Spoons are extremely versatile and can actually fulfill more than one job duty efficiently. You can eat liquids with them, eat solids with them, cut things with them if you need to, and are more important than a fork, which you cannot use for eating liquids. I'm a lot like that in my professional life; versatile. I can do more than one job efficiently.

WHY IS THIS BEING ASKED?

YOUR INTERVIEWER WANTS to understand your logic and response under pressure.

TIPS:

PROVIDE the best possible answer and how it relates to you in your professional abilities.

123.
Q: What would you like to be doing for a career two jobs from now? Do you think this job in any way will help you get there?

A: I want to be working for myself while running my own company. I do believe this job will help me get there, as there are important skills I will learn from this management position. I will learn how to properly and adequately deal with situations that arise every day, as well as how to manage employees more efficiently. (EXAMPLE)

WHY IS THIS BEING ASKED?

THE EMPLOYER WANTS to know what your long term goals are, and whether this position is something you are generally interested in.

Interview Questions and Answers...With Your Future Employer

TIPS:

FIND ways in which this position could relate to your 'dream job' and give reasons as to why. Two jobs from now may be a long time off, but give some idea as to what your thoughts are.

124.

Q: What was one of the most humorous things to happen to you in recent times?

A: (Provide explanation)

WHY IS THIS BEING ASKED?

DEPENDING on the position you are applying for, the employer might be looking for how personable you are. If your job duties entail customer communication and being friendly and upbeat, this question will show them a bit of your humor and how you dealt with the situation.

TIPS:

HAVE FUN WITH THIS QUESTION, and be honest!

125.

Q: Do you appreciate working in the company of others or would you rather work *with* others?

A: (Provide an answer depending upon whether or not this position is oriented at working alone or with other people. Be careful how you answer, here)

EXAMPLE: I prefer to work in the company of others, in my own cubicle, with the hustle and bustle going on around me.

OR

I MUCH PREFER WORKING with others or as a team.

WHY IS THIS BEING ASKED?

DEPENDING ON THE POSITION, this could be an important question. They want to know what environment you work best in.

126.
Q: Do you need complete silence when you work because noise bothers you, or do you like the noise?

. . .

A: I really do need silence to complete this type of job and do it right due to the concentration I need to complete my tasks.

OR

I DON'T MIND the noise at all.

WHY IS THIS BEING ASKED?

THE EMPLOYER NEEDS an honest answer as to how you work best. If you are surrounded by noise and need to have quiet to work, chances are the position is not for you.

127.
Q: If I gave you a choice between this job for the amount of money you proposed, or your dream job for less money, which one would you choose?

A: I would choose my dream job, definitely. Money is great, but working and being happy with what you do is even better.

WHY IS this question being asked?

. . .

CHARACTER QUESTION; shows your true colors.

TIPS:

CHOOSE what would be more important to you- the money, or the happiness.

128.

Q: Do you believe work should be fun, or it should feel like work?

A: I believe work should be a mix of both. I try to enjoy myself while at work, while understanding the seriousness of my position.

WHY IS THIS BEING ASKED?

THE INTERVIEWER IS LOOKING for personality based information about you.

TIPS:
State your honest feelings on the issue. Chances are, you will reply with something like the above answer anyway.

129.

Q: If you were any color, what color would you be? You don't have to say why.

A: I would be red. (Example)

WHY IS THIS BEING ASKED?

COLORS, believe it or not, say a lot about a person. They are trying to find out more about how you perceive yourself. Your answer will help them understand the inner workings of how you view yourself.

TIPS:

DON'T JUST CHOOSE your favorite color. Choose a color that represents who you are.

130.
Q: How are you with follow up calls?

A: I am always on top of following up with clients. I make sure I develop a system – or follow the one you have in place here – and stick to it, following up with clients and leads in a timely manner.

WHY IS THIS BEING ASKED?

. . .

IF YOU ARE WORKING in sales, especially, this is an important question. Be sure you state the fact that it's something you just automatically know to do.

TIPS:

IF YOU DON'T LIKE FOLLOWING up, you probably shouldn't work in sales. Follow ups source many new sales and even piques more interest than the initial phone call.

www.ingramcontent.com/pod-product-compliance
Lightning Source LLC
Chambersburg PA
CBHW052110110526
44592CB00013B/1556